# BILLIONS OF YEARS OF YOU

# Billions of

# Years of You

## ROBERT FROMAN

*Illustrated by Kathleen Elgin*

THE WORLD PUBLISHING COMPANY

CLEVELAND AND NEW YORK

Published by The World Publishing Company
2231 West 110th Street, Cleveland, Ohio 44102
Published simultaneously in Canada by
Nelson, Foster & Scott Ltd.
Library of Congress catalog card number: 67-13828
Text copyright © 1967 by Robert Froman
Illustrations copyright © 1967 by Kathleen Elgin
Designed by Jack Jaget

*To the staff of the 96th street branch*

*of The New York Public Library*

## ACKNOWLEDGMENT

I want to thank George Gaylord Simpson, Agassiz Professor of Vertebrate Paleontology at the Museum of Comparative Zoology at Harvard College, for providing the idea that set me to work on this book and for reading the manuscript and making invaluable suggestions for its improvement.

R.F.
*September 1966*

To make possible your existence, the whole world had to happen. You are the result of a long, long chain of events. The history of the universe is also the history of you.

In a sense you are only a few years old. In another sense you go back billions of years. And all that long stretch of your past is yours to relive in your mind. Each year scientists uncover more details about it.

Whenever you want to, you can relive as much of the time since you were born as you can remember or find out about. You can do the same with the lives of your parents and your grandparents and other ancestors. And you can relive the story of your country and the story of your civilization—the story of the human species and the story of animals in general, the story of life on earth and the story of the earth, the story of the solar system and the story of the great galaxy of stars to which it belongs.

It is all your story.

A year forgotten is like a year that never happened. One way to keep from forgetting the years of your life is to see how much you can remember by yourself. Then get someone to help you find out more details. Family picture albums are useful; sometimes an old photograph will suddenly release a stream of memories.

Your mother and father can tell you things about your past that you never could find

13

out about otherwise. They can also tell you about their own lives, the next step in the history of you. They can tell you where they were born, where they went to school, where they met each other. You can go on adding details for years and years past as you think of things you would like to know about them: What was you father's first job? Where did your parents live when they got married?

Your four grandparents' lives are also part of your history. They will probably enjoy telling you about themselves and about your parents and your aunts and uncles. You can learn still more by looking through old family letters and records, the kinds of documents professional historians use in their work.

Then come your eight great-grandparents. To learn about more than one or two of them will be difficult. Even more difficult is finding out about your sixteen great-great-grandparents and your thirty-two great-great-great grandparents. No matter how hard you search for clues, sooner or later you are bound to lose the thread of your family's history.

Then you can move on from the history of your family to the history of your country.



The history of America is the history of her immigrants. People are often surprised to learn that all Americans, including the Indians, are either immigrants or the descendants of immigrants. This is because the human race evolved in Africa and Asia and Europe. All the people of the New World came from the Old World.

The first to migrate were the ancestors of the Indians, who began crossing from Siberia to Alaska long ago when there was a land bridge across the Bering Sea. Much later, Europeans began crossing the Atlantic from

the northeast and Africans from the southeast. Still later, Orientals began crossing the Pacific from the west.

Not all Americans know exactly when any of their ancestors arrived in the New World or exactly where they came from. If you can get this kind of information about some of your ancestors, it will be part of your family history. But the history of your country is the history of all its immigrants, from the earliest

to those still arriving. You can go about claiming this part of your past not only by learning what you can about your own family's immigration but also by learning something about all the other immigrants and what they have done here.

Just as a person's family is part of something bigger—his country—so his country is part of something bigger—his civilization. Ours is called Western civilization.

Many ancient peoples have contributed to modern civilization, among them the Sumerians, the Jews, the Greeks, the Romans. We owe something to each of these: the formalization of a code of laws to the Sumerians, the Old Testament to the Jews, and a great many of our ideas and ideals and the very words in which we formulate them to the Greeks and Romans.

One of the basic ingredients of all civilizations was first developed by the ancient Egyptians. Before one generation could pass on its knowledge to the next, there had to be a way of making permanent records. Messages that are memorized and passed along

by word of mouth get changed. Careless memorizers sometimes say the exact opposite of what they were supposed to say. The Egyptians worked out a system for making permanent records. They invented writing. And with that five-thousand-year-old invention, history began.

5,000
YEARS
AGO

Writing is one of mankind's greatest achievements. Most of the knowledge we have and will acquire in the future exists only because of that invention. Until there was a way of making permanent records, each generation could pass on to the next only the few things that could be memorized.

The Egyptians, who invented writing, were among the world's first city dwellers. It was dwelling in cities that made possible the development of civilization. In fact, the word "civilization" comes from the same Latin root as the word "city."

Until about ten thousand years ago all men spent their lives wandering around in an endless search for food. In the crescent of hills

1  2  3  4  5  6  7  8  9  10  000 YEARS AGO

around the Mesopotamian plain the kinds of
food they found most abundantly were wild
barley and wheat and wild sheep and goats.
Little by little, men learned to cultivate plants
so that they would produce more grain and
to tame animals so that they would yield
more milk and meat and leather.

In the course of a few generations men were able to stop wandering in search of food and to settle down to producing it as farmers. It was this great achievement by our Stone Age ancestors, the development of farming, that made it possible for a few men to produce enough food to supply others who lived in cities.

But the inventors of farming lived before the invention of writing, so they could leave us no written history of their times. What we know of them comes from archaeology, the study of the relics of past civilizations—their temples, tombs, tools, pottery, weapons, religious articles. Yet from such evidence we can learn a great deal about the people of prehistoric times, enough to give us, with the aid of imagination, a pretty clear picture of how they lived.

In the ten thousand years since the invention of agriculture there have been endless changes in our ways of living. In the last hundred years alone, for instance, the United States Patent Office has issued patents on more than three million inventions, ranging from hairpins to rocket engines. And every year there are changes in clothes fashions. Both inventions and fashions are part of civilization.

But in the tens of thousands of years before men began growing food there were relatively few changes in their ways of living. One of the great changes was in the development of speech. Most animals can soothe or alarm or admonish each other with simple grunts and cries. Our ancestors were able to make a great variety of sounds, and eventually they

learned to string them together into words and sentences.

As the centuries went by, our ancestors also learned to make better and better tools. They chipped flints to make sharp spear points and knives. They whittled pieces of bone to make needles. They hollowed out stones by pounding them with other stones so that they could crush nuts and grains in the hollows.

There were hardly any changes from year to year and very few from century to century. You can get some of the feel of that distant part of your past by imagining a hunt, such as a hunt for a woolly mammoth, an extinct relative of the elephant. Not all men in those days hunted mammoths, but most hunted large animals of some kind. Sometimes they

drove their quarry over the edge of a cliff. Often they drove it into swamps or mudholes to slow it down and then attacked it with spears.

Of course, they did not just hunt for animals. They also gathered wild fruits, grass seeds, and edible roots. They kept looking for things to eat wherever they went, and unless they found something, they went hungry. In those days no one had to worry about getting fat.

Tracing the ancestors of our species is even more difficult than tracing our own great-great-great-grandparents. All men alive today are members of one species, *Homo sapiens.* Our closest living relatives are the great

HOMO ERECTUS

AUSTRALOPITHECUS

NEANDERTHAL MAN

apes, such as the gorillas and chimpanzees. But they are very distant cousins.

All we know about the other species most closely related to ours comes from paleontology, the study of fossil remains of life in the past, because the last such species died out many thousands of years ago. A fossil is any bone or other part of an animal or plant of the past preserved in earth and stone. Study of them can tell us a great deal about the buried past.

Just over one hundred years ago, for instance, a workman, digging in a cave in a gorge called the Neanderthal near Düsseldorf, Germany, found a fossil human skeleton that astonished the world. It had a big, thick skull, jutting brows, and a receding chin. Now we know that it, and hundreds of other fossils like it found since then, belong to a species or subspecies we call Neanderthal man. They probably were not our ancestors, but they were our close relatives.

Since the discovery of Neanderthal man,

fossils of many of our other early relatives have been found. Some scientists think that one of these relatives, who first appeared perhaps a million years ago and is called *Homo erectus,* may have been our direct ancestor. The australopithecines (meaning southern apes), who lived in Africa and perhaps in parts of Asia as long as two million years ago, were close relatives of our ancestors of that time. Some australopithecines had teeth and bones so much like ours that it is even possible they were our direct ancestors.

One of the most exciting developments to look forward to in the next few years is the filling in of more and more details of the story of the immediate ancestors of our species. Today, hundreds of scientists are working in many parts of the world to supply these details.

| | PERIODS AND THEIR LENGTH | TYPICAL DATE |
|---|---|---|
| CENOZOIC ERA (AGE OF MAMMALS) 60,000,000 YEARS | RECENT 5,000–20,000 YEARS | 12,000 YEARS AGO |
| | PLEISTOCENE (ICE AGE) 1,000,000 YEARS | 700,000 YEARS AGO |
| | PLIOCENE 11,000,000 YEARS | 13,000,000 YEARS AGO |
| | MIOCENE 16,000,000 YEARS | 25,000,000 YEARS AGO |
| | OLIGOCENE 12,000,000 YEARS | |
| | EOCENE 10,000,000 | |
| | PALEOCENE | |
| MESOZOIC ERA (AGE OF REPTILES) 125,000,000 YEARS | | |

PROCONSUL
13,000,000–25,000,000 YEARS AGO

Our genus, *Homo,* may be something like a million years old. It emerged in the Pleistocene period, the geological period of the ice ages when glaciers repeatedly pushed down from the Arctic over much of the Northern Hemisphere. We are part of another group that is much older. This is the superfamily of apes, men, and near-men called the Hominoidea.

Paleontologists have found fossils of many of our predecessors in that superfamily. These fossils are the remains of animals that lived in many parts of Africa, Europe, and Asia before the ice ages began. Some belong to the

Pliocene period, which opened about thirteen million years ago, some to the Miocene, which began about twenty-five million years ago.

During most of that time our ancestors probably lived in trees, much the way chim-

| | PERIODS AND THEIR LENGTH | TYPICAL DATE |
|---|---|---|
| CENOZOIC ERA 60,000,000 YEARS | RECENT 5,000–20,000 YEARS | 12,000 YEARS AGO |
| | PLEISTOCENE (ICE AGE) 1,000,000 YEARS | |
| | PLIOCENE 11,000,000 YEARS | |
| | MIOCENE 16,000,000 YEARS | DELTATHERIUM |
| | OLIGOCENE 12,000,000 YEARS | 50,000,000–60,000,000 YEARS AGO |
| | EOCENE 10,000,000 YEARS | 50,000,000 YEARS AGO |
| | PALEOCENE 10,000,000 YEARS | 60,000,000 YEARS AGO |

panzees live now. But toward the end of the Pliocene the great forests dwindled and were supplanted by grasslands. A few of the tree-dwelling apes ventured out into the open country and, little by little, over thousands of years developed the ability to live on the ground and to walk upright.

That accomplishment was of profound importance to us. One of the fundamental differences between men and apes is the upright posture. Walking upright freed our ancestors' hands and eventually made it possible for them to learn to make tools.

Sixty million years ago, in the early part of the Cenozoic era called the Paleocene, our ancestors did not look anything like us.

They were the early representatives of our order, the Primates, which we share with such mammals as apes, monkeys, and lemurs. In many ways they resembled modern tree shrews, which also belong to our order but are among the more primitive living mammals.

Those ancestors lived almost entirely in trees because it was not safe for them on the ground. There were too many bigger and faster animals that they were not yet clever enough to outwit. Then, too, they did not yet have thumbs like ours.

If you want to see how important it is to have a thumb that works the way ours does, try to pick up a pencil without using your thumb. You can do it only awkwardly, and you would have a hard time writing that way. Not until millions of years later, when our thumbs evolved so that they could swing around and oppose the other fingers, did we begin to learn to handle things easily and skillfully.

Our order, the Primates, belongs to a larger group of animals called a class. Our class is known as Mammalia, the mammals, and includes the animals that suckle their young with mother's milk. Besides our order it includes many others, such as those to which cats, horses, squirrels, and whales belong.

The first mammals evolved about 180 million years ago in the early part of the Mesozoic era. And for more than one hundred million years thereafter they were utterly insignificant. If you could take a trip back to that era in a time machine, you would scarcely notice these ancestors. The biggest of them were about the size of opossums, which some of them looked like too. But in those days the great dinosaurs dominated the earth. They were up to eighty feet long and

|  | PERIODS AND THEIR LENGTH | TYPICAL DATE |
|---|---|---|
| **CENOZOIC ERA** 60,000,000 YEARS | EOCENE 10,000,000 YEARS | 50,000,000 YEARS AGO |
| | PALEOCENE 10,000,000 YEARS | 60,000,000 YEARS AGO |
| **MESOZOIC ERA** 125,000,000 YEARS | CRETACEOUS (CHALK AGE) 10,000,000 YEARS | 100,000,000 YEARS AGO |
| | JURASSIC 25,000,000 YEARS | 130,000,000 YEARS AGO |
| | TRIASSIC 30,000,000 YEARS | 180,000,000 YEARS AGO |

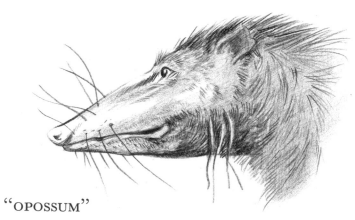

"OPOSSUM"

180,000,000 YEARS AGO

thirty tons in weight. To stay alive, our ancestors had to spend one hundred million years keeping out of the way of these enormous reptiles. They did, though, and eventually the dinosaurs died out.

Although the dinosaurs were not our ancestors, we share ancestors with them. Both they and we descended from members of the Amphibia, animals that lived part of their time on land and part of their time in water. Those ancestors did not look much like such modern amphibians as frogs and toads, however. They looked like fish with legs.

Until about halfway through the Paleozoic era, the time of ancient life that preceded the Mesozoic (middle life) era, nothing at all

| | | PERIODS AND THEIR LENGTH | TYPICAL DATE |
|---|---|---|---|
| PALEOZOIC ERA 330,000,000–335,000,000 YEARS | (AGE OF AMPHIBIANS) | PERMIAN 25,000,000 YEARS | 215,000,000 YEARS AGO |
| | | PENNSYLVANIAN 25,000,000 YEARS | 230,000,000 YEARS AGO |
| | | MISSISSIPPIAN 30,000,000 YEARS | 250,000,000 YEARS AGO |
| | (AGE OF FISHES) | DEVONIAN 50,000,000–55,000,000 YEARS | 350,000,000 YEARS AGO |
| | (AGE OF INVERTEBRATES) | SILURIAN 40,000,000 YEARS | 370,000,000 YEARS AGO |
| | | ORDOVICIAN 80,000,000 YEARS | 400,000,000 YEARS AGO |
| | | CAMBRIAN 80,000,000 YEARS | 475,000,000 YEARS AGO |

lived on dry land. A few primitive plants were the first to venture out of the sea and take up dry life. They were followed out by a few scorpionlike creatures. Then, about 350 millions years ago, certain fish that lived in the shallows developed the ability to breathe

ICHTHYOSTEGA, A LATE DEVONIAN AMPHIBIAN

(length about four feet)

in air as well as in water. This gave them a new way of escaping their enemies and helped them to survive dry periods.

To recapture that part of your past you need to imagine an earth on which many of the land plants looked like ferns or mosses of giant size. Few animals of any kind wandered among them. Clumsy though they might have seemed, the first of the air-breathing fish to go flopping out on the land on their stumpy fins were among the world's great pioneers.

43

We know that our class, the mammals, is about 180 million years old, but we do not yet know how old is a still larger group, called the phylum, to which the mammals belong. Our phylum, the Chordata, includes all animals with a backbone, or at

SEA SQUIRTS

least with a stiffening rod of some sort down their backs. We share this phylum not only with our fellow mammals but also with birds, reptiles, amphibians, fish, and certain other most unusual animals such as the sea squirts.

It is difficult to think of sea squirts as animals, let alone as relatives of ours. They look something like tiny barrels and live attached to the sea floor like plants. But in their infancy—called the larval stage—they look much like microscopic tadpoles and swim free until ready to settle down.

Some scientists think that our phylum may have descended from animals like infant sea squirts that lived perhaps six hundred million years ago. Others doubt this and are still looking for more evidence about our ancestors of that time. All agree, though, that the first members of our phylum certainly lived in water and probably in the sea.

These remote ancestors had nerve cords stretching above the stiffening rods down their backs. At one end of the cord was a

45

lump of nerve tissue. That lump was the meager beginning of one of the great wonders of our world: the human brain.

We chordates belong to one phylum, insects and lobsters to another, clams and oysters to another, earthworms to still another. But all of us belong to the animal kingdom. And we know that our kingdom goes back more than six hundred million years. Beyond that point it blends into the other great group—the plant kingdom.

The startling fact is that we have plant-like creatures among our ancestors. The most ancient fossils are of single-celled organisms called protists. These lived more than two and a half billion years ago. So far, they are the oldest known living things. And, of course, they had ancestors too. Even the tiniest protists are marvelously complicated organisms. One of the greatest accomplishments of modern science has been the discovery of how the first life on earth could have developed from lifeless matter.

The essence of that discovery is that atoms of different elements can, in certain circumstances, link together to form complex mole-

CHRYSAMOEBA

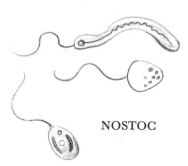

NOSTOC

47

cules that have the power to bring together more atoms to make more molecules. Long chains of molecules form in this way and develop the ability to put together other chains like themselves. This is how living things may have risen step by step from non-living matter.

At least one and perhaps two billion years before life arose, there was another event of considerable importance in your history—the birth of the earth. Our planet seems so big and permanent that it is hard to realize there was a time when it did not exist. But five or six billion years ago it may have been only a lot of gas and dust floating in space.

Astronomers are not yet sure how the solar system originated. Most think that the sun, earth, and other planets probably were born in much the same way that a drop of rain is born out of a cloud of vapor. They condensed out of that great cloud of gas and dust.

The condensing began perhaps six billion years ago or a few hundred million years

BIRTH OF A STAR

later. It was nearly complete by at least four and a half billion years ago. But many, many years had to pass before anything could live on earth.

At first our planet was just a jagged piece of metal and stone, something like a big meteorite except that it was red hot. Or, to look at it from another point of view, it was a great collection of chemicals in the process of reacting to each other. Heavier ones sank

50

toward the center to form the core, and lighter ones rose to the surface.

In the process, gases were released and assembled to form the atmosphere. Other gases rose, condensed into rain, and fell back to the ground. At first they instantly evaporated again, but eventually the surface cooled enough so that pools of water could form in low spots. The oceans began to form.

The first atmosphere, the first oceans, and the first surface of the earth were far different from today's. It took a long chain of chemical and physical processes to make the earth we know.

Our earth and sun and the other planets of the solar system are part of a galaxy. Our galaxy is the Milky Way, more than one hundred billion stars arranged in a great disk so broad that it takes light one hundred thousand years to travel from one edge to the other. Our solar system is two-thirds of the way out from the center toward the edge of the disk.

Just as the earth and moon travel together around the sun once each year, so the sun and its planets travel in a great curve around the center of the Milky Way. But the distance is so enormous that it takes 230 million years

THE MILKY WAY

for us to make a complete revolution. It has taken us ever since the beginning of the Mesozoic era—the Age of Reptiles—to make one circuit.

Vast though our galaxy is, it has not always existed. Today, most astronomers believe that, like our sun, all the other stars of our galaxy condensed out of enormous clouds of dust and gas. But they are not sure how long ago that process may have begun.

53

HORSEHEAD NEBULA

Recapturing the story of the first few billion years of our awesome galaxy is a little
like trying to recapture the story of the first
few years of our own lives. Indeed, it is even
more difficult to get details of what happened.
But astronomers and astrophysicists are learning to interpret echoes of events that took

54

place in the early days of our universe, echoes that still reverberate through time and space. Every year they discover fascinating new facts about the ancient period of our universe to help you reclaim that part of your past.

Sooner or later our minds turn to the wondering question: Where did the cloud of gas from which the stars of our galaxy condensed come from? And what about all the

other great galaxies of stars? We know there are hundreds of millions of them in the universe. They seem to be rushing off in all directions.

With such new ways of studying the universe as radio astronomy, and with the help of observatories on artificial satellites, and

eventually on the moon, we shall learn more
and more about the universe in the years that
lie ahead. But already we know that from the
origin of our galaxy to the thought in your
mind at this moment there has been one long,
continuous line of development. From dust
cloud to star to solar system to molecule that
reproduced itself to living cell to fish to amphibian to mammal to tree shrew to ape man
to ancient man to you—down through that
long line—patterns have been growing in
complexity.

The most remarkable result is what you are
doing at this moment   thinking. The greatest wonder is that in your thoughts that
whole long line lives again.

GALAXY NGC5128, 15,000,000 LIGHT-YEARS AWAY

# INDEX

## ABOUT THE AUTHOR

ROBERT FROMAN was born in Big Timber, Montana, and went to school in Caldwell, Idaho. When he was fifteen years old, he decided that he wanted to earn his living as a writer and after attending Reed College in Portland, Oregon, and working for various publications, he became a free-lance writer in 1945. Mr. Froman and his wife, author Elizabeth Hull Froman, live in Garnerville, New York.

## ABOUT THE ARTIST

KATHLEEN ELGIN, who has illustrated over thirty-five books is also an author. Born in Trenton, New Jersey, she studied at the Dayton Art Institute in Ohio and the School of General Studies, Columbia University. A wintertime resident of New York City, Miss Elgin makes her home on New York's Fire Island during the summer months.